Wings Fr...

Poetic Reflections of a Pastor's Wife, Mother and Educator

Debra Stanford, PhD

Cover design by: Art Painter

Library of Congress Control Number: 2018675309

ISBN: 9798711257226

Cover design by: Art Painter

Library of Congress Control Number: 2018675309

Printed in the United States of America

This work is dedicated to my daughter,

Deanna Stanford Tan.

Her life brings battles and victories untold.

Foreword

This book was created from years of experience and the need to find a voice to live an abundant life. It was developed from recording one thought at a time in journals to reflect the time and space lived in. I am grateful for every encouraging word given by my family members, teachers, and friends. I also extend a special thanks to Bettina VanPelt who set an example of courageously sharing poetic pieces and mentoring others.

Debra Stanford, PhD

"Finally, brothers and sisters, whatever is true, whatever is noble, whatever is right, whatever is pure, whatever is lovely, whatever is admirable--if anything is excellent or praiseworthy--think about such things." Philippians 4:8, NIV

Contents Title Page

Introduction

This book is a poetic and prose compilation of a series of events that occurred during my experiences as a young wife, mother, and instructor. There are key persons of my life that had I not had their support and prayers, I could have never produced such a grand display of my thoughts, emotions, and instincts. These persons include my loving husband, Apostle Joseph L. Stanford, my children: Joseph Jr, Mattie, Daniel, and Deanna. In addition, my wonderful church family at the Ambassadors for Christ World Outreach Ministries! Without the above-mentioned persons influencing me in my beliefs and faith in God, my life would not have been as victorious as it resulted.

"Wings from the Westside" is the title of most popular poem. It describes the history of children who manage to excel from poverty and reach affluence and influence. When I wrote the selections of this memoir, I was not a Doctor of Philosophy specializing in Curriculum and Instruction. I was the wife of a pastor (generally referred to as a First Lady) whose church was founded in the United States. We had launched our first international destination in Jamacia. Among other responsibilities, I was a former schoolteacher of the Chicago Public Schools, Administrator of a daycare called Little Lambs in Elkhart, Indiana and Executive Director of a non-profit community-based organization called Family Cares (AFC) Mission. Like many women who attempt to juggle work, church, and family; many times, I felt overwhelmed with responsibilities! Additionally, I had to face the challenges of being a mother with children diagnosed with a chronic illness called sickle cell disease of which we had no history of existence within my own or my husband's bloodline.

Nonetheless, everyone's lives unfold with challenges, but we must decide how to cope with the unexpected and still maintain our joy and peace. I questioned myself back then and asked, should I simply embrace difficult times with hopes and prayers, or should I find something within to excel above them? What task could I engage in that would help me feel more of a human being and less than a robot performing within a matrix that is programmed to do and be a certain way? My answer was through my writing of poetry and sharing it within my community.

As a teenage girl, growing up on the Westside of Chicago, I aspired to become a writer. I wanted to write novels that focused on romance. I wrote 2 novels that were read and critiqued by my English Teacher, Dr. B. Through Dr. B 's influence I was accepted in the Medill School of Journalism at Northwestern University. Later I changed my focus and became an English Major and minored in Education.

I married Joseph in 1984 and continued a career as a teacher. Not only was Joseph a wonderful husband, father, and pastor, but he was also an amazing businessman. Eventually, he would lead a small group of believers and establish four 5O1(C) 3 organizations of which I found myself involved in. In addition, Joseph always wanted a house full of children, so we raised 4 of our own as well as others within the church. As I reflect on it now, it was a type of Brady Bunch situation! I easily adapted to being mother with many children probably because I was from a family of six siblings. I loved motherhood, but after a while, I felt a yearning for more as an individual.

In 1999, I purchased an expensive journal for my budget and began to write in it often. I would leave the journal on the fireplace in my bedroom. I noticed that some evenings Joseph would pick it up my book and read a few pages. One night he said, "Baby, you are very good at this. You need to take some classes or join a poetry group to sharpen your skills and share your talent with others." I was surprised to say the least at his suggestion. Here is another task on my "To Do List."

I have always had confidence in my husband's judgment. Joseph had history of making wise decisions in ministry, business, and family matters. He wanted me to take this hobby of writing to another level! Soon, I joined a neighborhood writing group that gathered each week. I later discovered that the producers of this group published a quarterly magazine called "The Journal of Ordinary Thought" (JOT). I attended Columbia College and took a writing class. Soon I began to publicly recite some of my work in forums such as Chicago Cultural Center, the Palmer House, the Chicago Public Libraries and my own church, The Ambassadors for Christ.

Poetry had become more than a hobby for me but a catalyst of energy that propelled me to grow as an individual. It allowed me to let my voice be heard to audiences that were diverse, generally open minded and intellectual. I was able to share my writings with others and received encouraging feedback. Later, I discovered that within a 3-year period, I had produced over 100 pieces of artistic work! It was through this media that I felt inspired to begin my studies to receive a doctorate in education.

Although most of these works were written years ago, I   know that you find these pieces relevant for today. For many years, these writings were scattered in different settings that included my office file cabinet, my home file cabinet, boxes, and journals at home. It had reached a point where I had no intention of compiling them to be ever read again by an audience other than my children.

I am confident that this memoir is relevant to people of many backgrounds! Whether you are a mother, father, child, or inquiring individual reaching for a another means to connect to a higher form self-actualization, continue to turn these pages or scroll down. You will be transported to another place and time that will help transform you. I invite you to experience life and soar beyond obstacles. You can reach the goals in life that you never dreamed possible, and you can develop a sense of fulfilling your purpose here on earth. I encourage you to reflect on major happenings in your life through writing poetry, music, or any means of recordkeeping. And although you may not be from the Westside, it is a great chance that you have wings that can take you "far above what most could anticipate..."

Preface

These beautiful pieces of art encompass concepts that are motivational and inspirational. This burst of poetic energy can help to uplift and inspire those in search of a greater purpose in life. During times of mediation and prayer, I was inspired to write pieces like "My Spa" "Wisdom Flows" and "I Lay Before His Presence." Interactions with outstanding people in my life precipitated the creation of poems written about my father Daniel Watson and aunts: A Candle in the Dark, Bessie Collins /We Ate from Your Hands and Christine.

Enjoy!

Order of Poetry and Prose

Inner Transformation

I'm Brewing

Like a coffee pot

Which has been complete

With water,

Filter and

French Roast,
I'm brewing…

I've been turned on to

Share my thoughts and

My experiences

And the mixture of

Ingredients is culminating

Within me…

The fluid is slowly

Descending

And a fresh aroma

Is filling the air.

Hear the drip

Listen to the

Drop.

And know that

Something which was

Destined to come forth

Has now entered into your ears.

The Unveiling

Fatigue.

This has been my hinderance

This has been the culprit of my

Lack of adventure.

fatigue.

Far too long have you kept me

From exploring my true self.

Far too long have you enumerated

The things I have done for the day,

And given me reasons to blow out the candle and do no more.

You have prevented me from

Going beyond my natural abilities-

My day-to-day mediocre tasks

To exhibiting or manifesting the

Person who I really am.

I am a writer.

I am a painter.

I am a pianist.

Fatigue – today I renounce you!

No longer will you dictate to me

What I can and cannot do.
I defy you and declare

I am free. I am a spirit

I am a living organism that was design to

Blossom!

Blossoming entitles

Allowing words that are usually unspoken

To be spoken

Allowing thoughts to be heard which if

Not written would have been known…

Allowing colors to been seen that are

Inside of me and if I never handled with a brush

Would never be seen.

This Blossoming

Allows the music inside of me to

Explode and bring forth

Sweet melodies to the listeners.

I have taken a deep breath

And counting silently to three

To finally reveal the person

Who I really am;

A Journey

I am on a spiritual journey

A journey that is substituting

Paths that I normally

Would travel.

Sometimes, I don't realize

The direction that

These roads are taking me

But every once in a while

I am enlightened and I see

That I am going places that I've

Never gone before

Places that I had visited previously

Are now secondary

Compared to the ones I'm

Going toward today.

The people I'm meeting

Are of diverse backgrounds

And many cultures.

This is a wonder to me.

Because I always thought

The usual was The Way.

Somehow, I can imagine how

Dorothy

Felt

As she traveled the yellow brick road.

She was full of excitement and

Much anticipation in her quest to see

The Great Wizard.

But instead of a wizard

I expect to see Christ…

Welcoming me with open arms and saying

"Well done my good and faithful servant."

How Is Your Cup?

Are you able to drink the

Beverage that has been put before you?

When you sip it

It tastes delicious, doesn't it?

Drink a little more and

That taste good too.

But at some uncertain point

Or sometimes

Definitive point

You experience an

Aftertaste

Then a

Bitterness

That doesn't quite well agree with you.

Your eyebrows draw together

You look puzzled and ask

How is this possible?

How can something sooo good

Change to become sooo distasteful?

You look within yourself.

You look within the scriptures and inquire:

Have I sinned?

But Jesus answered those who had questioned him

In reference to inquiring of the blind man

"Who had sinned his mother or his father?"

"Neither. It is for the glory of God."

"Here. This is your cup.

Can you drink of its contents and still love me?

By the way…

What's in your cup?

Is it sickness?

Is it disease?

Is it poverty?

Is it death?

Is it failure in relationships?

The contents of yours

May be entirely different from your

Sisters or your Brothers.

Even its color may vary from black,

Brown, blue, orange, yellow or red…

Nevertheless,

The cup that each of us possess has a bitter

Taste that makes it

Difficult to digest.

Some will refuse it.

Others will not.

Our test is to:

Finish it with a smile and say

"Thank you, Jesus."

How is Your Cup? Part II

When you have been through

Mazes

Of pain and suffering

It's easy to realize that there is a force

Within the universe

Far greater than yourself.

Your spirit can get weary and

Practically die.

But no one around you –

Except those closest to you

May know.

Although your eyes may be burning

From stress and/or lack of sleep

The world seems oblivious to your

Bloodshot and haggard appearance.

Even your mode of dress has changed

In that you project simplicity and comfort:

Sometimes wearing the same

Outfit 2 or 3 days in a row!

Are you invisible?

Is the world callous?

No.

Only blind to your state of existence.

You are having an encounter with an

Invisible God

Of which only you and he can settle.

This is the

Substance of your cup.

Realize that as you drink its contents

Allow the medicinal ingredients to

Flow into your mouth

down your esophagus

and into your belly.

It will ultimately go into your

Bloodstream.

Like natural food

It will give you nutrients and vitamins

That you need to grow as

A person.

Reject the thought of regurgitating;

Binging has never been acceptable.

Take it as a remedy

Or as the cod liver oil

That you had to take as a child.

Can you remember the effects?

Can you recall the smell?

It helped to change you!

You were healed.

And now, more profoundly,

You are transformed!

You are not the same person

When you digest the contents

Of Your Cup.

Your experience has allowed you to

Have a closer walk with your maker.

The benefits within your cup

Far surpass the pain and suffering you endured.

You have entered another

Realm of reality.

There are truths you had held so dearly

Of which you now see clearly were

Not truths but speculations and perceptions.

Your window of

Wisdom, Knowledge and Understanding

Expands through the experiences

You have within your cup.

Congratulations!

You have entered into a world called

Life!

My Spa

If you can find a place of solace in me

Welcome!

If my physical existence in this earthly world

Can project a spiritual enlightenment

And help you temporarily forget

Some of your problems

Have a seat.

If I can create a type of music that makes

A tune of which you can relate

Sit back and relax.

Isn't it wonderful that we can distance

Ourselves from our everyday

Mundane routines to partake

Of something

Worthwhile, self-satisfying and innocent?

How powerful are our minds that can

Transform us in and out of situations

And totally abandon realities!

If by this time I have showered you with

A moisturizer of

Grapefruit, mango, peppermint or vanilla...

You can totally surrender!

Now, feel free to enjoy

A full body wrap, massage, and reflexology

During you appointed time

In my spa.

The Conversion

I have consumed you in my thoughts

Your ideas

Your lives

Your memories,

I allowed you to speak to my

Mind for countless hours.

I was influenced by you in

Some form or fashion.

Lorraine Hansberry

Langston Hughes

Richard Wright

James Baldwin

Maya Angelou

And even

Shakespeare.

You talked to me when no one else would.

You were my friends

Who revealed to me concepts

Of life that I had

Never conceived.

Actually, you were my escape

From reality.

I understood you clearly.

But when I reach for a spiritual uplift

And placed my hands on the

Holy Bible

I was confounded.

I sought meaning but found

No interpretation.

Was this book only for

The Preachers and the Priests?

Or was it all gibberish,

Nonsensical or non-applicable

To modern day situations?

I became frustrated and practically

Threw the tablet away as

Moses did on the mount.

Time passed…

I tried to ignore it

But my curiosity would not

Let me stay away

Too long.

Another day, I turned the pages

And frustration resurfaced!

Again, and again I tried.

But finally, one day

After Christ had revealed himself

To me and came within my inner being

And placed a quickening within my belly

That was far beyond my imagination

I opened the Tablet and

Understood his holy language

Christ words jumped out at me

Unlike any other piece that

I had ever experienced!

His truths

His parables

His acts

His love

Surpassed that of any other

Prophet that I had ever known.

And then a hunger and thirst came

That drove me to read the Holy Bible

Every chance I got.

I literally digested it by

Memorizing verses

And dissecting it chapter by chapter

Scripture by scripture

Until…

I loved it

I believed it.

I consumed it.

And

I am living it today!

I Lay Before His Presence

When I find that there

Is nothing more that I can do

I lay before his presence.

When I lay before him

I am surrendering my

Mind

Soul

And body

To be subject to

His will.

I release all authority that I

Thought I once had

And cry out to him for

Help.

What am I but a

Speck

Of all of his creations?

I have no power only

Energy that he invested in

Me.

He developed me from

My mother's womb

And knows my

Innermost being.

If I cannot subjugate myself

To him my life would be full of

Misery and pain

When events fail to unfold

In the manner that I anticipate.

Therefore, I lay before his presence.

I utter prayers that are

Incomprehensible to man

But he knows.

I weep.

Not necessarily because

I'm sad but because

I am yielding to a power

That is vast, grand and

Magnificent.

Where is my pillow?

Where is my quilt?

I need to stay before him

Longer.

Total Surrender

Overtaken

Dear Sweetheart,

When I felt overtaken

You lifted me.

When I felt driven

You seized the controls and

Secured me.

Without touching me

You shook me into reality.

You are more of a man of God

Than I could have ever imagined!

You have planted

Seeds within me that I will

Nourish

Cherish

And

Share.

To my darling husband…

Seizing the moment

Like a camera

That's used to capture precious moments

Of life

I use my pen and paper to

Seize the moment

As I am inspired by

God with words.

I must capture those moments

Of revelation

Which are given to me at

No set time of day or night.

This is a part of my spiritual journey.

I must freeze thoughts

With pen and paper

And as I write

More thoughts flow and are brought into

Written form.

Before I know it,

I have seized another moment

Of Listening to "I am"

Which is proving to

Strengthen

Revitalize

And

Increase faith!

Beauty Choices

"Your hair is too short for that style"

After your third appointment she asks:

"What did you say your name is?"

"You look really tired today."

"You look like you've been through a lot since I last saw you."

"I don't have any magazines. Maybe I can borrow One but *You* have to return

It to Vanessa."

Your stomach growls. You're hungry but on the wall a sign reads:

"No eating nor drinking in this facility."

Luci defiantly states:

"I don't do braids.
I don't wash braids.

I don't do curls and please don't ask

For waves."

You watch the clock as

Minutes pass…

Then hours…

Luci gives you a mirror

You force a smile

Reluctantly, you each for your purse.

You looked better coming into her

Than you do going out!

But then there is Priscilla…

She treats you special because you are!

She prepares you for those special occasions.

She literally lays out a red carpet for you as you enter her

decorated shop surrounded with elaborate furniture and flamboyant curtains.

Priscilla greets you will a big red smile that you know is authentic!

You return the smile even though yours is forced because you are

exhausted from the events of the day.

You look worn.

You feel worn.

You are worn.

For the entire week you have served everyone but yourself.

Priscilla escorts you to her big chair and gives you a copy of

Contemporary Coiffeur and then asks:

What can I do for you today?

You want to scream

"Just make me beautiful!!!"

But you know you need to be more specific than that.

You slowly turn the pages of the magazine knowing that whatever

Style you select

Priscilla can duplicate!

Whether your hair is

Long, short, curly, straight, damaged, thick or fine

Priscilla can quickly give you

Braids, French twists, curls, wraps, weaves or waves!

Priscilla's hands are those of a skilled artisan who can transform

Whatever is set before her. And her speech...

Her speech is gentle, encouraging and loving.

You find the style from the magazine and she replicates the fashion

Nice and Easy.

And when she is finished, you look in the mirror and

Voila!

Your first thought is "Who is this?" You wonder if someone else

Entered the room...

Those scales of burdens that you arrived with have now

Seemed to have disappeared from your countenance and

Your spirit.

You look younger.

You feel younger.

You look prettier.

You are prettier!

You smile.

Priscilla helped to restore confidence in you that you

Hadn't realized was depleted.

You question the theory that "the way we look is only one percent of who we are."

You reach for your purse and reward Priscilla generously!

You exit the shop and are now ready to conquer the world!

Pastors' Wives; Is it all Rosy?

They see the gold.

They see diamonds.

Can they feel the pain?

Do they have an inkling of your suffering?

"Your clothes are lovely. The coat fabulous!"

Should you tell them the real price you paid?

I laugh within when I hear a young woman look at

The glory of a pastor's wife and exclaim

"That's what I want to be one day!"

Little does she know that

This woman had stayed awake practically the whole night

Counseling and consoling

A mother who son had just been shot

A friend whose daughter had taken an overdose of drugs

A father whose child had been hospitalized with a chronic disease.

The Pastor's wife does not regret her position

She reveres it because it is a calling from God.

Unless born into a pedigree of pastors' wives'

She had no idea that the union to one man

Would mean a unity to many, many more.

She had no idea that the words she uttered

Could greatly influence those around her

Whether good or bad.

She had no idea that the burdens her husband

Had not yet taken to God concerning

Someone's else's life

Would sometimes lay between the

Two of them at night.

Pastors' wives, I salute you.

You who have stood the test of time

One year or twenty.

Always remember that your smile

Projects a beacon of hope to all

Within your circle of life.

You are indeed

A queen

And 1st Lady

Because you represent a brilliant jewel

Abiding in The shepherds' house.

1st Lady Dozier

Salt

I need ¼ teaspoon of salt to make

1 serving of oatmeal.

½ teaspoon of salt is needed for a

Pot of spaghetti that can feed a

Family of 8.

It takes 3 tablespoons of salt to season

16 lbs. of greens.

Did not Christ say that

We are the salt of the earth?

Since this is so

What a great impact a few of us can have

On our fellowman if we simply open

Our mouths to proclaim his goodness!

Matthew 5:13-16 "You are the salt of the earth. But if the salt loses its saltiness, how can it be made salty again…"

Celebrate!

Now it's time to rejoice in our mates.

Already we have rejoiced in the

God of our salvation.

The time has come for us to

Recognize, appreciate and shower love

Upon the one who

God has joined us to.

Let the emotions we have

When we are alone

Transcend to other settings.

The unity God created between

Us is more than physical.

It is a power to be shared with

Our children

That will transmit into all our affairs.

If we only value that distinct

Moment of ecstasy

By secluding it, bottling it and

Putting it on a shelf-

We miss the essence of the beauty

That God intended.

These flowers…

This cologne…

This is only a token to

Let you know,

I celebrate my life with you!

Oprah

Queen of modern times

Blessed with beauty

Intelligence and wit.

Through your charism

And love for people

You manage to break

Barriers of prejudice

Stereotypes

And preconceptions.

I watched you on

Television and marvel at your

Free and refined spirit.

I survey how it is like a magnet

Even to your competitors.

Oprah,

I feel a kindred unity

Between us that makes me proud

You are my sister.

It's it interesting

How that we still do not know

So much about ourselves and yet

We can detail the lives of others?

Yet despite all odds

You rose to the top!

In you I find hope that

One day

I too will represent life and

By the grace of God

Instill faith that can

Improve lives and

                  Change destines!

In the meanwhile

Oprah,

I pray for you.

I pray your strength

I pray your happiness

I pray that the virtue you

Share will be

Replenished unto you and

Dispersed among others.

He Added

When it looked as though

He would take away

He added.

After the alarm went off

And

There was a rush to save

That which was threatened to

Be stolen

God added.

Through the rise of blood

Through the sweat

And through the pain

He added another experience to

Your hope and he added faith

To all who knew…

He added…then multiplied your blessings.

The Story

I can only tell part of the Story.

The story about life and life's issues.

The story about coming face to face with reality

And learning with your eyes wide open about

God.

God's requirements of our faith can come down so

Suddenly

Like a judge who first seemed indecisive about a matter

Then slowly appears with his black rode and gravel.

He then hits the hard wood for silence and pronounces a sentence that

Was not anticipated and cannot be disputed.

He is the Supreme Court and an appeal is impossible.

But behind God's stern countenance there is a love for you that exceeds that

Of any other.

But at the moment, he appears to be the enemy. Just as our parents appeared to

Be unfair in their pursuit to raise us to become responsible individuals.

Yes, sometimes we can choose paths to take in life with diligence and

Arrive at our desired destinations. We become doctors, lawyers, entrepreneurs,

Teachers, writers and preachers, or find that perfect partner!

But within those paths are cracks and crevices that made those

Journeys difficult and at some points, the entire success of the mission was

Questionable.

And within those cracks and crevices are the Stories.

The stories could be tales we don't want to utter but a moment that could possibly save

The life of someone else who has been sentenced with a similar term.

The Bible states, "There is nothing new under the heavens…

And this is true no matter how unique our problems may appear.

Let's share.

Let's give another hope to make dreams less remote.

And because no one shared their stories with us, we should be even

Compassionate.

Although we may tell the story, we will never tell all.

Your story made you become more aware of the

Fragility of human existence.

Beyond Borders

The Rose of Innocence

The Rose was found in a newly cultivated garden. It was surrounded by petals intact and craftly displayed. It was also found among thorns and thistles. As expected of roses, it had a perfumed fragrance but this one was so red that it could be seen in the dark.

The Rose of Innocence had fellow companions that all had their unique characteristics. Some stood upright, some were bent towards the north, south, east, and west. But they all smiled at the sun and the sun smiled back.

Then a visitor came. He desired the rose although he knew it was forbidden. He looked around to see if anyone was present and removed it cautiously so as not to prick his fingers from the thistles. He detached the rose from its stem while using his left hand to balance the vine. Like a giant seizing his prey, the visitor pocketed the innocent rose and swiftly walked away.

The pocketed rose still appeared alive but is now summoned to die.

Returns

How can we plant seeds of love

And receive returns that we never imagined

Possible?

Whether the fruit is good or bad

How can the factor of extreme be so

Prevalent in life?

The answer is that God created the seed

Cultivated the fruit and we are only here as

Stewards.

Therefore, we should not

Glory in our victories

Nor faint in our trials –

This is God's world and

He makes all things well!

Something was Lost

Through those dark trials and

Tunnels of pain

Something was lost;

A song

A poem

laughter.

Troubles altered that bright

Outlook of life and caused

Happiness to cease deep within.

Yet on the surface

An aroma of joy

Seeped through your existence.

That desire to

Create

Develop

And expand

Was smothered.

And when the pain did cease…

Scars remained that continuously

Reminded you of your suffering.

Only though the knowledge of Christ
Did you survive.

Your consolation came through
Knowing the good that Christ did
And the pain
That he suffered
Far exceeded any mishaps and
Disappointments that you
Endured.

And though something was lost
God can restore
An abundance of everything
Far above your imagination!

Battles vs Solace

Battles come in all forms and sizes

We can be engaged in more than

One battle at a time.

It's very disheartening when those battles

Enter our dreams.

Reality can be a battleground when

We tread on surfaces of

Social settings, children, marriage, education,

Employment and health.

But when we close our eyes, we expect to

Rest.

When rest flees and other spirits dominate

We must surrender to God and

Believe in his word

Where he said

"…I'll never leave you nor forsake you." Hebrews 13:5

Colossal

You are…

A colossal of a man

A definition of a man from

The crown of your head to

The soles of your feet.

You are…

That giant statue of a man

Of which other men must go underneath

In order to reach their destines.

They look up to you

Acknowledge your greatness

And then proceed successfully to

Their goals.

You are the configuration of a man

A creation designed to become one of

God's companions:

A manifested son!

To God's Anointed

When we water down

His messages

We dilute the power of the word.

We are trying to mix

Vinegar and Oil

Which we know cannot be maintained.

We are including

Ice to glasses of orange juice or milk.

We have added liquid to a

Solution which is already

Packaged and ready to use.

This is like adding

Flour to a box of cake mix

Which needed only water and eggs.

Hence:

We dilute the power

We divert it from its purpose

We nullify its effectiveness.

Jesus is worthy of all

Honor, Glory and Praise!

This House on a Peninsula

This house

Is the kind of house that

Couples dream about

But never actually live in.

As I sit in my bedroom

Looking from the window

I can see the river being enjoyed by the white swans.

There are several trees and bushes on the landscape.

The water from the river gives an hypnotic effect

Which causes me to feel a

Release of burdens, cares and concerns.

Schools of brown ducks look like those that for years

I had only watched on TV.

 Before today I didn't know the smell of the countryside

Nor the breeze of a clean atmosphere:

Only the city winds and pollutants.

I can now view nature from my bedroom window

Firsthand!

Tears well in my eyes as I meditate on

I have been fortunate to experience so

Many good things in life.

And you, Joseph

Have been the catalyst of most of the events.

You have the creative eye to see

Beyond the natural

A faith to believe that anything that

God has for us will be

Acquired.

Our children can enjoy the grass and birds

Surrounding our house.

I can even glance at them every now and then

From my kitchen window as I

Cut up green peppers, onions and tomatoes that

Seem fresher here that our other abode.

Although my stay may be

Only for a season.

I am grateful to be awakened by

The sound of a geese

Rather than

A tooting horn

A fight in the night

Or a false alarm.

Oneness

A feeling that you are flowing

In the will of God.

A delight to be in the sun

And not feel irritated by it.

Instead, you experience comfort

In its rays and

Somehow feel akin to it.

Oneness…

An apparent control of time and events

A peace

That lets you know that you are not alone.

Oneness…

Is what makes others look at you and

Wonder

"How can he or she do it?"

An Inferno: Contemplating on Dante's

Going to hell and back is not such a remote idea if you have tried to rescue someone or free yourself from the snares of the devil or as some may say "strongholds". Battles involving sickness, death and torn relationships are most prevalent. In hell, all that first seemed to be imperative, suddenly lose their value -gold, silver, houses, cars…When in the inferno, food becomes an absolute necessity as an attempt to escape the pain and endless aggravation. There seems to be no foreseeable escape. Your journey appears an endless night.

There is a burning that only you are aware of and even if you tried to describe your plight, others still cannot imagine the intensity. Fellowship is basically useless and can often worsen the situation. The inferno demands solitude, much meditation and prayer.

Prayer? But your prayer is only a whisper, your knees are no longer conditioned for kneeling and your spirit is shattered. Therefore, you basically stretch on the floor and hope that God will have mercy and come to strengthen you.

And he does…In the moment you least expect, angels come and fortify you. They enable you to go one more minute, then hour, then day…

The flames are still alive yet somehow you are walking within them as the three Hebrew boys walked through furnace -but then someone said four. Mechanically, you find strength to still carry on routine responsibilities while trapped in coals of fire. Others marvel at your courage but you know that the hope and energy you have is supernatural. You keep walking for the sake of not losing everything. And before you know it, before you could have guessed…The inferno is behind you!

Smoke is in the air, ashes lie here and there, but how insignificant this is compared to the torture of the flames. You smile. Trees are greener, the sun is glowing with hues of yellow and oranges that you never had noticed until this day. Nature was never more indulging, nor the sound of laughter and the sight of children playing.

You have experienced that which was before unknown, dreaded and far- fetched! But now you know you can live! You can make it! You can survive; even through an inferno!

Lights, Camera, Action!

But there were no lights

There was no action.

And if a camera was somewhere nearby

A photographer would not dare to use it.

The Ambassadors for Christ World Outreach Ministries

Was holding a Tent Revival in

Long bay, Jamaica.

This is a rural area where poverty dominates.

The generator had broken which meant

No electric power could be found.

No microphones

No speakers

Nor keyboards

Could operate.

So, what did they do?

What had they done?

Most had walked over 2 miles on the dirt road

In the heat of the summer evening.

They were weary from their journey and hungry

For a movement of God's spirit.

They had come to worship with a ministry

All the way from the United States of America

And believed with all their hearts they would be

Blessed.

Like robots they sat in the front rows of

The aligned wood chairs:

Adamant that they would get what they came for.

The lead man, who they called

Apostle Stanford asked:

"Should we cancel this service?"

They said in unison:

"No, Apostle Stanford, we want to have service."

Minutes passed and still

No light, no camera, no action.

Apostle Stanford now rephrased his question:

"Do you want to go home?"

Again, they responded mechanically:

"No, Apostle Stanford, we want to have service."

Their tenacity and earnest desire seemed to have

Shaken heaven because suddenly

There was a beam of light in the direction of the

Pulpit.

Everyone looked for the source.

Headlights from a red raggedly Oldsmobile lit up the tent.

The Americans could now see a glimmer of

The churchgoers faces.

Most looked like them;

With dark complexions and bright eyes.

But their kinky, braided hair and sometimes worn and dirty clothes

Distinguished their homelands.

The artificial ray of light and

Precipitated some smiles.

And then

Suddenly

The floodlights beamed

The speaker echoed notes from the

Keyboard and melodies resounded.

Those Jamaican soldiers

Clapped their hands

Danced their holy dance and sang,

"God is a good God."

But this was only the prelude!

On Jamaica Praise

There was a fervency is his praise that was

Unlike any other.

He beat that tambourine as though it was connected to

His own heart moving towards abundant life!

He raised one leg while he stomped the dirt floor

With the other.

His eyes were tightly closed as though he could see

Something that he didn't want to lose.

There was a rhythm in his dance and a freedom in his spirit

As he circled the pews singing with the congregation.

Sometimes, he would stop and scream instead of sing the words

To the song "Jesus, I love you."

His words resounded throughout the room and those who

Witnessed his actions could not refute his claim.

It was too obvious;

His praise would take him far beyond the Jamaican border.

He was destined to reach shores unseen and glorious!

Ocean's Tides

They left their footprints

Deep

Within the sand.

But the ocean's tides came and slowly begin to wash away

Traces of their length

Traces of their width

Traces of their breadth…

The ocean's tides were strong and released a mist grand

And marvelous…

The ocean's tides roared like a lion ready for its prey.

The ocean's waves became higher and fiercer than

The waves before

Until finally

The ocean's tides had erased the imprints

In the sand and scattered every grain

Onto the ocean's floor.

And after being scattered on the ocean's floor

Each grain of sand

Dispersed more and more until

Every particle that made up the whole was totally

Independent of the other.

And when we came to see the deeds that had been done

On the ocean's shore

There was no trace

There was no hint

There was no jot

Of what had been there before

And yet we know that those prints had once

Lived.

We could almost swear at the points where

The prints lay.

But all traces of the footprints were gone.

Each grain of sand had been lifted off the

Beach and scattered…

The tides kept coming in

The tides kept touching the shore

The tides kept sweeping the sand until

Those impressions on the shore were absolutely

No more.

Scales

These scales of worldly entrapments
Must come down!
I must shed my physical existence
To allow the true and spiritual part of me
To come alive.

These scales have hidden me and
Tied me down to focus on the nonessential
Rather than that which is significant.
I shall not wait until the natural metamorphosis takes place
But I must accelerate the change and
Peel off these hard, stained scales
In order to promote
Beauty from within!

Masterpiece

How vast and marvelous you are

To care for all of which we care.

To sit at the bedside of each of us

Within all seven of these continents!

You cause thee rain to pour

And the thunder to roar

And suddenly

Stop and let the birds sing for joy!

How vast and marvelous you are

To put music inside of those tiny creatures

Who beckon us to arise from our beds

And rejoice with them at the dawn of a new day.

Masterpiece #2

There was a burst emitting from the sky

Then a clear sound of thunder.

Suddenly, the earth was covered with rain.

All greenery and perfume scented flowers had

Nothing to do but remain in places

While the creator nourished them.

And so, it is with us.

Wings from the Westside

Yes. Some of us develop wings.

Some of us are victims of circumstances, born in poverty, born in dilapidated buildings, born in filth!

Yet, some of us develop wings to fly. Wings that are strong and enable us to fly high.

We fly high and manage to go far…far beyond our natural habitat…for above what most could anticipate…

Our place of birth was simple. Our upbringing was painful. For many of us had no fathers. And many of us had fathers who were there in body, but not in spirit. They had allowed drugs and alcohol to cloud their visions and prevent them from sharing wisdom of survival and growth.

And we saw our mothers cry. Cry because they wanted to keep the family together. Cry because there was not enough money to pay the rent…Buy the groceries, buy the particular presents for Christmas that we had requested. Yes, some of us saw these deficiencies and still managed to fly out!

We had wings that allowed us to ignore the fact that although we were in school, how could we possibly compete with other children around the world where the ratio of teacher to student was 1:15 or less but the ratio in the ghetto was 1:30 or more. And still, some of us developed wings that would allow us to go around the world.

Some of us had the Eagles' Eyes where we could see so much farther than what was before us. We could see it and believe that we would make it to that remote oasis! We made choices. Choices that were not always the best, but we learned from those mistakes.

Throughout the years we exercised our wings. We flex our muscles and stretched our bodies and one day decided to fly. At first, we looked like we were on the same level as our neighbors. But slowly we excelled, we propelled and then we gained momentum. While they cannot see us anymore, those from the other corners of the world do. They wonder,
Where did he or she come from?"

We smile and say: "From the Westside." We don't have to tell them that we flew because the distance is so far from where we started, it's obvious. It's like making a trip from the U.S. to Japan. In no way can we get there on foot! They already know. We have wings!

Wings that enable us to be promoted in our present state and make us rulers:

– Kings, Queens and Presidents!

Wings from the Westside

Part 2

And our wings took us places…

Like the feathers of a peacock

Whose beauty is hidden until

It is aware of onlookers

We spread our wings to display

Such magnificence

That we could fly in all types of atmospheres.

Our hues were formed as we engaged our

Minds in areas beyond out sight.

At first, we discovered states,

And then geography took us to countries.

We engaged in virtual reality before the term

Ever surfaced!

At first, we looked like we were on the same plane as our

Neighbors.

But slowly were excelled

    We propelled

        And then we gained momentum.

While they cannot see us anymore

Those from the other corner of the world do

They wonder, "Who is he or she and where are they from?

We smile and say:

"From the Westside."

We don't have to tell that that we flew because

Our speech and looks betray us.

We were foreigners but have become citizens!

We have wings.

Wings that enable us to be promoted in our present state

And make us rulers –

Even over them!

Living Vicariously

Marathon Before the Masterpiece

Preparation Time! Change of everyday attire to that of compete comfort: cotton and spandex!

Exercise gear is placed from head to toe- some Nike, some Reebok, some Champion, Headband,

Wristband, Fruit of the Loom and Jockey Underwear!

Stretching is highly recommended prior to the race to loosen muscles that have aged and tightened with time. Stretch again with Yoga and Pilates.

On your mark, get ready...

Suddenly the sound o the bullet breaks the air...

Off you go...

With confidence you appear qualified to win.

A huffing, a puffing, a pushing forward define your being. Beating against the atmosphere and defying self- you finally approach the finish line and number one!

Cheers, disappointments, and surprises fill the air. Regardless of past perceptions and projections, no one can refute that you have now become

A Masterpiece.

Stretching

I am s t r e t c h I n g...

Stretching beyond my natural limitations.

Growing farther than what mind and body assumed.

Stepping forward when I initially stopped.

Doing what I thought of...finally!

Reaching for what I knew was there but felt was too high to accomplish.

Replacing wasted energy with something worthwhile.

Extending my former self into someone else.

Making my life meaningful to the point of unique.

Meeting a challenge with will and courage!

Roller Coaster Ride

Stigmatized...

Roller coaster ride

Categorized...

Roller coaster ride

Ostracized

Roller coaster ride

Pre-judged

Roller coaster ride

Seen as many...

Labeled with

Limited expectations...

You took us on a journey

Untold and never imagined

A ride that diverted from the norm...

But what is norm?

We all go some type of

Roller coaster ride...

A ride that is unexpected and takes

Us away from the matrix.

Our hearts pound...

Our blood levels rise

Our eyes nearly pop from

Their sockets...

The hairs on our heads stand upright…

And the only fear is the next height and angle we will

Be found in.

But each ride has its own theme

Its own purpose.

Like the snowflakes' designs

And like the uniqueness of our very fingerprints.

What matters is…

The state we are found in

When the ride stops.

Meeting the Storm

Rain sifted liberally to earth.

Lightening flashed sporadically.

Thunder roared and then challenged

Her to enter the arena.

Slowly she arose from her poise of comfort

Slipped on a red jacket and reached for her keys.

"Will she actually and deliberately

Partake of this battle? Or will she suddenly renege and lose all confidence

As she had done before?

The intensity of the elements heightened

Sounds were louder and more forceful than before.

Her walk hastened. She would not turn around.

All her natural body pressure emerged with the atmosphere

Chill, wet and an overall discomfort became part of her demeanor.

There was a burn, an itch and even outright pain…

But she kept walking forward as though she felt and feared nothing.

And she kept defying natural instincts until

The rain subsided

The lightening ceased

The thunder quieted and then

The storm passed. She evolved.

She was tough but still a lady

She had discovered another realm of living

And although the sun had not yet revealed itself,

She glowed.

Chicago – The Windy City

The wind…

An unseen force that effects both

Animate and inanimate objects.

A drive that pushes and pulls without

Regard of rank, status or history.

Supposedly…

And so, Chicago lived up to its name.

Heads were disarmed as hats, scarves and earmuffs were

Stolen by the east wind.

Clothes were opened, torn, tattered and ripped apart as

Certain ones desperately attempted to keep them in

Place.

But there was no savoring.

There were no farewell parties…

Instead, there were cries and screams

Of disbelief that roots could be

Uplifted, displaced and finally abandoned

So mercilessly.

There were feelings of helplessness

Hopelessness and outright resentment.

Imagine you…

Were one of the children torn away from friends

At school and in your neighborhood despite the

Opposition of your parents…

Imagine you…

Were a member of that YMCA now boarded up to

Be demolished, where years of your

Leisure time was spent on the gym,

At the pool and in the game room.

Isn't it interesting how the wind swept away

Everything the Westsiders knew in all directions

But east, downtown, Rush Street and Hyde Park?

If we listen closely, echoes of the voices of those

Blown away can be heard on a windy night…

Goodbye teacher…

Goodbye mentor…

Goodbye friend…

And the wind still lives up to its name…

Running rampant, running high, running cold, runny breezy.

A Candle in the Dark

I see my father…

When I see a man working by the sweat of his brow from sunrise to sunset

Refusing to rest until the job is done.

I see my father

When I see a man, quiet, unassuming and trustworthy.

I see Daddy…

As a man inwardly frustrated with life – with in invisible resume outlining a third-grade education of boasting several years of experience on the cotton field.

But when I knew him, he worked long hours at the factory, throwing leather from one machine to the next and after aging struck, promoted as janitor; cleaning toilets and emptying garbage cans laced with beer, pop and sometimes vomit.

At sunset Daddy would come home to us seven, then six children, his only biological son was killed while chasing a ball in the street.

We were siblings of very different interests. One in karate, two in song, three in computers, four in guitar, five in writing and six in so many, many questions about life.

I see my father trying to escape some the misery this life presented…searching through the maze of strangers, associates and those he lived to feed, and yet always arriving at a dead-end.

His hand-carved outlet could not be against the integrity of this family…

For he was indeed a father…

He was indeed a faithful husband…

He was indeed a diligent laborer…

His outlet had to be against himself.

Secretly he made his weekly visits to the man who legally gave him the thrill for his life. The man who was clean cut, poised behind the counters majoring in brands of cigars, cigarettes, whiskeys, vodkas and wines. But Daddy's special were Schultz beer, Camels Cigarettes and Hennessey Whiskey.

And Dan was systematic. Always purchasing enough for 7 days- 5 evenings plus 2 full days of uncensored pleasure. His supply will be wasted by Thursday night and replenished by Friday – Payday!

Despite his will power for righteousness in all other areas, this habit was unbreakable. Year after year, day after day he indulged.

Until finally…He met a man who eased his worries – a man who talked to him in the evenings and

Satisfied his thirst for life…

A man who became his real friend…

Taking him places he had never gone

Pointing out the beauties of life he had never noticed –

Then allowing him to feast on delicacies he had never sampled.

Dan met Christ – who stood up in him like a giant!

For although Dan remained quiet and mild mannered

He had a love for people that projected like a candle

Lit in the Dark.

Wisdom Flows

Suddenly you find yourself in the middle of the Atlantic Ocean

with only a bathing suit and surfboard as your gear…

This must be a nightmare! But it is your reality!

You were indifferent but now prepared to stand upright to fortify

Yourself to meet the tides.

The next moment, you enter a crest of waves

That appear to be prepared to swallow alive

Any object that would dear to confront them.

How fierce that beautiful water has now become!

The mist of the waves shoots at your face, your chest,

Arms and legs like arrows meeting

Their targets in a round of archery.

But you steady yourself to maintain the sudden

Lift of the waters….

Soon you find yourself flowing atop.

One moment ago, there was a mass darkness,

But now you stand on that surfboard with the blue waves

Beneath you and the orange sun above you.

You lift from your crouch to steady yourself

While the wind combs through your hair and causes it to

Respond like gestures of applauds. You smile. Not out of pride but out of pleasure.

Yet you know He has nothing to prove to anyone.

You manage to stay composed as the waves descend.

Finally, you slowly kneel to the surface of the board.

You excel, relax and then impulsively scream

As you glide toward wet but steady sand.

We Enter Their Worlds

We enter their worlds

When we sit and focus on that one-eyed screen.

And allow our minds to become entrapped into

Scenarios of fabrications, hyperboles and exaggerations.

We become accomplices to lies, deceits and make believe

And allow our emotions to sway with the tale-

Experiencing an array of sensations from love to hate

And sanction unmerciful revenge for our heroes.

We practically become a part of the character that beats then murders an offender

And a half hour later fall in love with Leonardo DiCaprio and Julia Roberts.

We find the man or woman of our dreams

Meet the challenges of

Man vs. man

Man vs. nature

Man vs. himself

And momentarily live happily ever after!

We consume the airways, hoping to escape from our ways

But we always come back.

Reality slaps us in the face and say

"Deal or Die."

Most of us chose to deal, but the channels

We select offer only two outcomes

Eternal life or eternal damnation.

The sensations in these places are different from that on

The one-eyed screen:

They cannot be turned off nor censored.

Why Dress Up on Sundays?

Why dress up on Sundays?

Why dress up at all?

Why do you select some of our finest attire for certain occasions?

Why do we decided to be casual in others?

Why do we dress up for

Job interviews

Court appearances

First dates

Graduations and

Proms?

Why do we go through all the trouble in matching this with that?
Buying gold, silver and sometimes

Diamonds (or custom jewelry) with blending shoes and purse?

Is it to impress even though the prices we pay is exhausting?

Is it to make ourselves have a better self-esteem, even though we
know we are spending far beyond

Our means?

Is it because everyone else is doing it, even though we claim we
are independent thinkers?

Or is it because this has been what we have been trained to do
since childhood?

Whatever the reason…

Dressing up should be a choice.

We should not allow it to become a demand.

To be clean, well-groomed and spiritually attuned is all we need on Sundays.

But since we have already invested in those three-piece suits, sequence dresses, long silk scares

And overflowing hats, let's not allow those pieces to mold or deteriorate in our drawers.

For then we would be like that wicked and slothful servant who buried his talents and

Consequently, found himself at odds with God.

And those stunning high heel shoes…

They're knock-outs but many times hurt our feet and feel so uncomfortable! Let's throw them away or

Give them to another with warning…

And the rest of those aching heels that we must keep

Wear them 2-3 hours or for the duration of our service or event

And like Cinderella-lose them on our way out of the door!

Whatever we decided to wear on Sundays

Remember God's eyes penetrates external surfaces

He can see right through our souls.

He knows exactly who we are, not matter how

Polished we may appear!

Bessie Collins/ We ate from Your Hands

How can we forget your hospitality?

How can we forget your love?

How can we forget your patience?

You were the queen of the family who: had much and gave much to everyone

You knew.

You opened the door to your home for

Family Reunions, Bridal Showers, Baby Showers, Parties and

Even Weddings?

On any given day, you fed us with whatever you had for yourself;

Fried catfish, cornbread, white rice and collard greens.

It seemed as though you were the only one who could put sugar in everything

And it tasted delicious!

I remember you ordered a pink suit for me from a Sears catalog. Weeks later it

Came in the mail, 100% polyester and it fit me perfectly. Today we would compare that

To ordering an Apple watch on the internet! I thought you were brilliant! No one had ever

Done this for me before and I wonder…

How many other items you ordered and purchased for

Your other nieces and nephews?

Your children, grandchildren and friends.

I sometimes spent the night at your house, slept in your bed and tried on your mink hat, mink stows and jewelry. You only smiled!

Touring your house was like walking through the pages of an

American dream house; Everything matched, everything was modern, everything was classic

And everything was clean!

You even had guestrooms that you lavishly decorated.

You loved life heartedly and was not afraid to share your life with anyone. You loved your church family at Greater Union Baptist Church and enjoyed cooking

For them as well as soliciting members. Everywhere you went you were a servant and a

Leader of leaders-but now that you are in your senior years, there is a single plant in Your bedroom window…Don't feel sad because you can't remember everything. -your relatives and friends have also forgotten much!

Aunt Bessie, we still love you. Thanks for the many years you greeted us with a smile and opened yours hands to feed us.

From Earnestine's daughter

And all of us who recall your generosity

Rebirth

Wanted 1st Lady

Ability to be exalted and abased simultaneously

Ability to serve cheerfully 15-20 hours a day

Ability to smile even when in pain.

Ability to speak nothing good of herself but of

Her husband with all sincerity.

Ability to overhear a conversation but not hear.

Ability to adapt to unforeseen circumstances with grace.

Ability to be in love with God more so than

Anyone or anything this world has to offer.

Any volunteers?

Where are the Roses?

Claudia became determined to find the roses.

When all she could see before her was darkness.

She reached for the petals and imagined that the

Soothe silky surface would kiss her fingers

But her effort was to no avail.

Claudia attempted to gather the petals in her fist

But all she could feel was a breaking of

Dried, dead particles that gave no promise to

Adhere for another second.

There was a faint echo of laughter that prevented

Her from hearing any music or calming silence.

Her sense of smell heightened to compensate for

The failure of her other means of knowing...

But when an odor did surface, the likeness of

Sour milk permeated the air.

It all felt too unending, too unreal and too unlikely to occur.

And still it did. She would not awake from a dream

For this was life in its rawest sense.

And through her blind search Claudia crawled on

Her knees to scramble for a morsel of hope

When suddenly Christ appeared

Rage

The breaking of glass and crystal. The creaking of wood from the wreckage of

Furniture tossed to and from. The sound of babies crying who were awaked by the

Carnage. Screams. Footsteps running for cover. A night always wanting to forget and

Never wanting to remember.

What other words can describe this scene but "Rage."

It was a reaction against the loss of his love. It was his way of self-expression. It was his way of venting.

What feeling can cause fearlessness?

What feelings can cause foolishness?

What pain can cause hatred?

It was rage.

What can promote such anger as to cause one to trespass?

What can promote such anger as to cause one to destroy?

What can promote such anger as to cause one to jeopardize his own safety

And the safety of the one he claimed he loved?

Rage. Uncontrollable. Illogical. But still Responsible.

And afterward…It was a war zone of a man

Who fought against himself

And lost.

To Richard

Through your selfishness and unforgiving spirit

You buried the friendship you had

Far beyond six feet.

Not only did you bury it

But you killed it by spreading

Lies and innuendoes that were

Irrelevant and unprofitable.

You destroyed something that

Was of more value than silver or gold!

You terminated laughter that could have occurred

And fellowship that was as sweet as David and Jonathan's.

You changed the course of destiny that was offering you

Uninhibited sharing and Ultimate caring.

You lowered the quality of your own life

And now privately regret that you took this road.

Maybe, if you repent

God will be merciful and restore to you the joy

That you once freely indulged.

Now…Pick up the phone

And attempt to make an investment gone wrong

Right.

Hearing the Drums

I can hear the beating of the drums...

This is taking me far, far away into distant lands.

As the drums beat my blood rushes upwards

As though ready to meet with a kindred spirit.

As my blood and my mind

Become totally enveloped in this resonating sound

My muscles begin to move in different directions

Unknown to me.

But my blood

That which distinguishes me from everyone else

Is composed of mixtures of men and women.

It tells the story of who I am.

The sound of the drums is like magnets to

My inner being.

My soul reaches upward

For them as desperately as those sound waves are reaching

Down towards me.

I can't sit still.

I can't be quiet.

I must meet this calling and if not

I deny my real self.

The sounds of the drums beckon me to

Refocus my attention.

They cause me not to be content with ignorance.

But to want to become

In fellowship with those drummers.

I am their heritage.

They are my forefathers.

Will I ever reach the goals that they intended?

Will they accept my suffering as an excuse

For my failure?

How much more would they have expected from me?

The Drumbeats Still

The beating of the drums echoed the

Pulsation of my heart.

They spoke to me in a language of

Which only the elements of my blood could understand.

The beating stirred a restlessness of which I was unfamiliar.

Simply because of the void of my knowledge of who I really am.

And yet my heart knew.

My heart longed to meet those who held the

Drumsticks that spoke to my soul.

What did they want?

What could I give them?

The pounding of the drums now became comprehensible

And defiant:

"Justice"

But how? How can justice be rendered where

Time and space have covered the identities

Of our offenders?

"They know."

Because their blood too is stirred by

The sounds of these drums.

When they raped my mothers

And lynched your fathers

They left their prints in the soil

They left their blood in the pot

That boiled of innocence and pain.

They will understand these drums.

They will repay.

The final sounds of the drums caused

A smile of relief to come upon me.

My heartbeats begin to settle and an

Easiness defined my composure.

Those drumbeats "I thought are fading.

Is my mission over or is there more?"

God's Response

To the Offenders of the Drummers

The repercussions of your sins

Influenced generations

Caused pain and agony of

Souls that left deep scars

Where no plastic surgeon can correct.

The repercussions of your sins

Divided families

Belittled individuals and separated

Mothers from their newborn children.

Children who became ignorant of their

 Brothers, sisters, aunts

Uncles, cousins and

All their real kin.

The repercussions of your sins

Changed the names of a people

Already given reputable names

And manipulated their way of living.

The repercussions of your sins

Stole the offspring of kings and queens 'and

Other dignitaries and mixed royal blood

With common.

What a devasting effect?

What unsightly deeds multiplied?

What pride?

The repercussions of your sins

Will no longer be silenced.

But restitution must follow.

Restitution is only what is right!

Truth

As liquid gold is poured from a transparent pitcher and seals

Whatever is placed beneath it

So is the truth which stands on its own.

Truth presents itself uncovered while lies

Are wrapped in layers of deceit and fraud.

Even truth's name is pronounced

Singularly

Whiles lies originate as one then

Multiplies as time progresses.

Truth stands alone and holds us up

but lies must be propped, stacked and are still unsteady.

Truth seals circumstances needing no excuses nor explanations.

Lies open inquisitions, inquires and curiosity

While simultaneously allow sickness and disease to germinate.

Truth can be painful

Causing facts to slap us in the face

And demands a courageous reaction.

But lies can be deadly

Causing fiction to erode our minds and damages

Our sense of judgement.

Truth is like a virgin teen age girl

Lovely, pure and flowering like a rose that is

Unplucked from a bush and glistens of crystal

Bathing in the sun.

Lies emit the stench and the sight of a rodent

That has been captured and punctured to

The death as it lays undiscovered for

Seven days.

And in its attempt to make music, lies make

The noise of an amateur drummer with no

Sense of repercussions, pressure or rhythm.

But Truth resonates as lovely song like a

Symphony of different sounds, intonations

And beats that takes us on a journey

From where we are to the place the

Composer wishes us to go.

Truth!

Najaw

(a dance troop)

A legend within legends.

A messenger sent to tell stories

Of those marked as black...

Stories that attempt to shed some light on

Our bleak past and give us some sense of

our identities.

For we, so called African Americans are

Not just from Africa

But Israel, Egypt, Jamaica and elsewhere...

Not necessarily created by mutual consent and therefore

Having bloodlines which only DNA can confirm.

Najaw...

How profound your mission is!

Teaching our children their heritage

Training our children to focus their minds

On issues that are meaningful.

How important your mission really is!

And those of you she mentored...

How fortunate you are!

Shedding light on darkness.

Spreading life where there is inactivity.

Guiding minds towards the betterment of a people deprived.

Najaw…

You are truly loved!

Christine

A jewel of the Nile…

So precious that we can

Only touch the glass surrounding you.

You are a sparkling pyramid of

Rainbow colors textured of triangles

And toppled of gold.

So pure, so honest

So meek and so mild.

Quiet yet powerful enough to

Subdue the roars of lions and yield

The necks of giraffes.

Christine.

Reserved for someone special.

Preserved for someone unique.

Your touch

Your smile

Your laugh

A jewel – lost in an ocean of beyond

And found on a beach of proximity.

Beholding you is a pleasure…

Knowing you is a sheer delight.

To Be or Not to Be

Pilate

A man noted for having the power to proclaim judgement but inability to execute it.

You had power that was in essence, powder.

While secretly attempting to obey the advice of his wife who stated "Have nothing to do with that just man" …you literally washed your hands to the challenge.

The crowd summoned you to perform and unlike King Saul, you stubbornly refused to participate.

Later when approached by Jews who wanted Jesus' grave bolted secure, you remained consistent and said "You do it"

The irony of your actions is that although you did not want to be blamed, you are because you failed to free an innocent man: Jesus Christ.

Others

History could have been altered had the actions of one man been different. And your actions also have an important effect upon the state of your environment. Instead of imitating Pilate by saying "You do it". Let us take a defiant stand for what we believe and what we want. Let's not deceive ourselves and say "We are innocent" or "our vote does not matter" when in fact we are as guilty of that Roman statesman. Let's simply magnify our voices to emancipate our brothers and sisters and ultimately free ourselves.

Poetry

Is such a spiritual process

That its ability to reach past

Religious boundaries are astounding.

It can somehow unite folks from the past

With those of us here today.

It is color blind where it sees no skin complexions

And is nonincriminating because it hears no foreign accent.

Poetry

Is like the sound of music that can be interpreted by

Americans, Europeans

And

Africans.

Poetry feels

Poetry smells

Poetry touches

Its characteristics can mesmerize and cross borders

Of age, upbringing and financial status.

It literally has a healing effect

When

It is permitted to be shared by

The Poets.

Geneva

Lake Geneva

Your blueness aligns with

The color of the sky

Hovering over Wisconsin

Because of the slight distinction between

You and the clouds, the horizon is almost hidden.

Your waters are still and yet

There is life within you that draws men

To your shores.

You have a heavenly glow

And a refreshing air that's calming and serene.

Your waters look like a sea of glass

That men can walk upon and never sink.

To view you once was not enough

So, my spouse and I returned to

See you again and to re-experience

Our thoughts and cares being sifted and blown away.

Focus

Let us emphasize

The beauty of life and place

The suffering in parenthetical form.

Let us enjoy God's blossoming creations

And pray for the blemished.

We should focus so much on those things

That are True, Honest, Just, Pure and

Lovely

Where those things which are the

Opposites are only shadows.

Sometimes we need to stand

In the shadows of suffering and even

Transform into this darkness so that

Our perspectives of life are expanded

And we are move appreciative of

God's favor upon mankind.

"For I consider the sufferings at this present time are not worthy to
be compared to the glory that is about to be revealed to us and in
us" Romans 8:18

Encircled by Roses

If my husband could have

Allowed me to live in a bouquet of roses

I believe that he would have.

He would have surrounded me

With red roses accompanied by

Plenty of ferns and baby breaths to

Let me be as comfortable as I could

Possibly be.

His provisions would have been

Somewhat different from that of God's.

Who decided that my life

Should encompass some pain.

God decided to put me in the

Midst of a bushel of roses.

Roses of every color,

Red, yellow, pink…

Yet protected by thorns and thistles.

These sharp and prickly objects

Are there not only to guard me from

Outside invaders

But to shield me from Myself.

They represent the tests

And trails of life

That prevent me from becoming

At ease in Zion.

It Beckoned Me

As I was exiting my bedroom early one morning

I was engulfed by a strange spirit that summoned me.

There was a presence in my room that beckoned me.

It beckoned me to stop and return to bow my knees in prayer.

It beckoned me to talk to God and somehow promised that

God would talk to me.

What an unusual encounter that sealed its calling

Within the confines of my mind.

I now believe that "it" was an angel

Reminding me that more so that

School

Work

Or play

I must acknowledge God's grace and give him the

Time that he so rightfully deserves.

Celebrate Part 2

Once again

I celebrate my life with you.

More so than years gone past

For within each year encompassed days

Where the sun could not radiate enough and

The nights where the moon's stillness could not

Calm the storms within me but you still held me.

I celebrate your years of maturity

Where you heard from God to help me mature.

I celebrate your love for me and our children

Despite all you have seen in

America, Jamaica, South Africa and Zimbabwe.

You return to us and

Hold me like no other…

You, Joseph are a light in my world

And a beacon of hope to everyone you touch.

You are a chosen vessel of God

And I am blessed to have you pass by me

Continually…

A Decree

An emancipating

A peeling off

A change

A transformation

A transfiguration

A metamorphosis.

A Renewal –

This is what God is now

Demanding of my character.

I must decrease and allow my mate to

INCREASE!

Some would laugh at this and state:

"She has always put him first."

Yet that discerner of the thoughts

And intents of the hearts

Has pierced me and divided my soul

From my spirit to help me to see

Who I really am.

Now I proclaim my F r e e d o m!

Refining

Tools of refinement are

Blunt like a hummer

Sharp like a chisel

And cutting like scissors.

They are excruciating!

We are part of the potter's plans who

Makes and molds vessels of clay

Then suddenly destroys the formats

Only to remake them again into the

Design he desires – regardless of its level

Of attraction to mankind.

The pressure from all the handling

And fashioning

Give us the substance to be versatile and compassionate

When before we were cold, still and unmoving.

Refining purifies Gold.

Refining also results in a more elegant vessel

In God's eyes than what we could have ever

Imagined.

Kiebessy

Near the end of the summer

I bought a plant called

Kiebessy.

Its leaves remind me of elephant ears –

They are thick and large for its height of

One foot and there are small pink flowers

Throughout the width of it.

To care for it the directions read

"keep moist and in sunlight"

I placed it near my bedroom window and watch it

Almost every day.

Somehow

I wasn't expecting the flower to keep blossoming

As the weather turned cold.

But in November

I noticed a fresh batch of pink blossoms

In a section facing east.

This discovery pleased me because if it

Is still blossoming in the fall

The chances of it blossoming throughout

The winter is very likely.

I thought about myself and how

That now I am at an age of maturity

I'm blossoming...

I've blossomed in my latter years

Where many my age are in a state of

resignation and anxiety.

I thought of Sony Bono – Cher's late husband.

And how he during his latter years

Behaved like Kiebessy.

At one point of his life

Situations looked dim and hopeless

But during his senior years he was

Elected a senator and died at the age

Of 62 while skiing.

Presently,

Within my writings and my artwork,

I too am skiing.

I am flying in the air

Feeling light as a bird

And enjoying God's creations even the more!

What a wonderful way to go!

Time

If spending lots of time together

The only factor lacking in our

Relationship

I dare say that there is no lack at all.

What is time but a measure

Designed by man?

The hours we spend together many instances

seem like days and the nights

We stay awake communing

Appear to be an extension of an era.

In God's eyes one day is

As a thousand and a thousand days are

As one.

And in the game of sports we savor the few

Minutes of overtime

More so than the usual allotted play.

And so it is with us.

What we do with our time is what's

Significant and what excites me.

You know and I know.

And no one else needs to know.

Inside of Him

(to the mesmerized pastor's wives)

Get from

Being inside of him.

Stop focusing on every move

He makes and

Concentrate on your own gift!

Be the woman that God

Intended you to be and

Stop

Lurking behind his shadow.

Grab hold to the key of Trust.

Will this guarantee the oneness

That you always wanted?

No.

The only absolutes are

God's stability

And

God's integrity.

He will not lie.

Stop!

(to the young ladies who envy the pastor's wife)

Stop looking at your spiritual mother and wishing

That you had what she has.

Stop allowing spirits of envy and jealousy to dominate your train of thinking.

In all honesty, do you know exactly what she has?

Are they only things that you can see?

Good looks?

Nice clothes?

Luxury car?

Beautiful home?

Designer Jewelry?

A husband who adores her?

But what prices did she pay?

Was it all paid with dollars and cents or were intangible currencies attached?

Perseverance?

Humility?

Longsuffering?

Relationships?

Temperance?

Your mindset is like a belief of achieving a fit body without exercise and a proper diet. Did you know that behind her smile and apparent desire to do everything perfectly, she has been through hell and back?

Although she had this...

And gone there...

Your spiritual mother knows that without God

She could not have survived.

Melody

The impact of seeing her was like

That of an arrow piercing through the

Center of my heart.

There was a sting, an ache and a

Urge to scream but then

a demand to be silent.

How foreign she looked as she lay on

The hospital bed.

Even her eyes were like that of a stranger

But there was a slight connection.

Her eyes

demonstrated a longing

For someone, somewhere, to somehow

Emphasize with her and understand her

Present state of dependence.

Melody lay there diagnosed with cancer with

Tubes traveling from her mouth to her esophagus and going to

Her belly. She was being nourished with Ensure

But somehow Ensure did not appear reliable.

Despite her present state of deterioration,

She had been a contributor of life.

Her name itself "Melody" allowed her to

Enter a room with a spirit of praise and laughter.

She was full of optimism, hope and joy!

Melody was my childhood best friend.

Although separated by time and chance,

We would sometimes gather for an occasional chat

To give updates about work, family and God.

Melody was still like a human flower that

Never withered or faded.

Physically, we grew apart –

Separated by gardens that yielded diverse ornaments

But are united by the same instructor of music.

Wings from the WestSide

A Final Salute

They mixed their blood with

Our blood

Then claimed that we could have

No part of them.

They sold our mothers

And belittled our fathers

And wonder why we wear of face of low self-esteem.

They burned our homes as well as our churches

And visit our neighborhoods with disdain.

They gave us obsolete textbooks and put our

Children in one room shacks

And now report that they are academically handicap.

No wonder they are overwhelmed when we excel

Above the rest!

No wonder they are weakened to their knees when we display

A backbone that could have only been formed by the Divine.

The Divine that called the children from the Westside to

Position their wings -

Arise and fly high.

Africa – A Reunion

My love went beyond the borders of our world
And entered Africa.
A land of fantastic stories of which
His heritage is thought to have abided.

He stretched his wings and flew into a land
He thought he'd never face
And upon arriving discovered
His royalty recognized
His dignity upheld
His righteousness revered.

He went and returned and
Continues to go there.

How can I compete with such attraction?
His memories of me will soon fade as
His mind is expanded and he discovers a
New array of people and another way of life.

As he changes, I must change.

I must hurt. For change is like the

Metamorphosis of the butterfly as it

Transforms within the cocoon.

Change require a solitary state of concentration.

It's like to state of the eagle where she plucks

Her wings to make a nest for her young.

I must will to change.

And as I am transformed, I will conform in the

Beauty of that region. I will fit into the picture of his

Present life where we both will soar into the blue

Skies of our motherland.

Our children will run with the Africans.

And become reunited with those of their kin

In body and in spirit.

Africa – A Reunion Part 2

My love goes beyond the borders

Of our world and enters a land

Once foreign and abstract – Cape Town South Africa.

Returning to the US is a duty for him

Except to those he loves.

Cries of those suffering with AIDS,

Empty stomachs of those in poverty

Spiritual deprivation of the chosen

Haunts him as he attempts to

Enjoy the luxurious of America.

This rare fascination,

This apparent addiction

Caused me to wonder if I too had been abandoned.

Had our years of private and public fellowship been

Only superficial? Or was there a hidden agenda of his travels?

Now he assures me that he speaks of me each day.

He injects his healing properties to those in need

And includes a dose of me.

They know my spirit

They know my works

They feel my longing

They await my arrival…

He has published me in a land I've

Never seen and one day present me

As his Afro-American Queen.

Africa -A Reunion Realized

Beautiful is the word the sub-describes

Cape Town, South Africa as Table Mountain decorates its land.

Humbled describe the attitude of those who can now

Roam about freely

Park their cars legally

Eat where they can afford

And travel without a pass.

Empty are the stomachs of the children whose

Fathers line up in the streets with signs begging

For work.

Awaked paints the picture of those who had been

Programmed to believe that blacks are inferior to

All other races.

Only 10 years.

Ten years of so-called freedom from apartheid and

Yet so much damage had been done that a healing must

Exists somewhere…mentally, spiritually and emotionally.

But where?

Where hope is alive. Where optimism abides.

Where those who were once destitute and forsaken

Have somehow excelled and met the challenges of life.

They Africans long for more Mandalas

More leaders to give of themselves unselfishly

And annihilate unfair political structures.

The Africans long for

Champions, heroes and heroines of

Their descent

Their color

Their suffering.

And as they stretch forth their hands for

Tangible examples of today

Let us look past our obsessions, excesses and

Abundance where we can see their eyes more

Clearly.

They we can reach to gravitate to them

And bring them to levels of unimagined dreams untold

And hopes once forbidden to utter.

And they the reunion will take place!

A reunion that will celebrate our long awaited

Journey of body and spirit as the day

When Mandela was set free after 27 years of

Imprisonment. Where millions of thousands rejoiced

Throughout all continents.

Smiles, laughter and relief describe the day of his

Returning. It was a reunion recognizing one man

But call forth others who will dare to arise!

Africa – love you…

One

The firebrand came down swiftly and was caught with a tight grip before touching the ground. He swirled this object and danced to the beat of the drums.

He wore a variety of colors, yellow, red, blue and green with the feathers of a peacock along with a tomahawk that signified the tribe he belonged to.

Skillfully, he hopped on one foot and then the other – denoting the passion he had for his music and the love he had for his heritage.

So, if he loved his heritage, how could he mingle with another?

With closed eyes, he could see her. He could see her dark mahogany skin that glowed in the sunlight.

Moreover, he could see her beautiful brown eyes, wide, far apart and alert enough to recognize any prey!

That slim dark body danced with the music of the tribe that came from another world – Africa!

It was not just the uniqueness of her skin color, but the spiritual aroma she projected whenever they neared each other. It was as though she had a special connection with a god of which he was unfamiliar but wanted to somehow get to know.

She flowed to the beat of her heritage, with a tambourine that seemed to highlight her existence and refine the already exuberant music!

The music was alive, it was real, it was her…

And yet, so much had been taken from them both…

The final beat of the music resonated and when he opened his eyes, she was there. The moonlight made her dark brown body glisten and her eyes sparkled with excitement! Her only desire was to be loved.

Her beauty and his desire for her company caused him to forget who he was, where he was from, and what others might think.

In silence, he reached for her. She submitted.

And soon they became one,

The heritages mingled and became a powerful force

Found only in the New World.

To My Mother: Earnestine Watson

Epilogue

My relationship with Christ has strengthened since the writing of these works. I remember telling the group facilitator of the "Journal of Ordinary Thought" Annie, that I had enrolled at Capella University to work on a doctorate, and she looked at me in amazement. There was something in her expression that made me feel that I would never return. Even though it was my intention to keep coming to the class, I was unable to. The inspiration that I had for poetry was replaced with reading and research. For seven years, I focused on my doctorate whenever I had any time available after my normal workdays and personal responsibilities. Finally, in 2014, I graduated Magna Cum Laude. This was an accomplishment that I had never even imagined. Whenever I reread "I'm Brewing" I realize that I was inspired at that period of my life. Had I not captured those words on paper, they would have forever been lost in an abyss.

My husband, Joseph, continued to encourage me in my efforts to acquire a doctorate as well as build my career as a community activist as he established churches around the world. Jamaica was the first overseas location and then we planted churches in other regions. For over 20 years, Joseph flew over to Cape Town, South Africa, and developed leaders to help spread the gospel of Jesus Christ. He is still working hard to help people be transformed into the likeness of Christ. He now has our older daughter, Mattie Stanford Johnson as one of his administrators. Additionally, Samantha May, who is a citizen of South Africa holds a vital role in the success of our overseas ministries.

My quest for a doctorate did not start until our youngest son, Daniel was a junior in high school. When he witnessed how well I was doing as a student, his grades improved. Now he is living in Texas as a data analyst for a community-based organization and is married to Andre.

My eldest son, Joseph Jr., has always encouraged me in my efforts as an artist. He purchased a picture for me years ago of a woman walking blindfolded on water and said that the woman remined him of me. Joseph Jr is a part time singer, writer, and entrepreneur of a flourishing gun range business in Chicago.

Finally, my youngest daughter, Deanna. She helped me to find the real meaning of motherhood. She is witty, highly intelligent, and very challenging in numerous ways. My experiences and interactions with her in the areas of health and education helped me to reach more to God for peace and assurance. It is her life that helped me to advance my relationship with the Father. While I looked for her to change, I learned that I needed to change! Today, Deanna is happily married to Carl Tan. Carl is of Filipino descent.

All the above persons helped to shape who I was then and who I am now. I am also grateful for God restoring relationships with my siblings of the Watson and Powers families as well as my childhood friends who lived on Washington Boulevard. What I am going to achieve for the next phase in my life still needs to be revealed. I am willing to continue to submit to the father and be open to whatever plans he has in store for me.

Only one poem was written in the group setting at the JOT. This poem was "The Unveiling". This poem was written on the first day of my attending the workshop and I was indeed fatigued from the happenings of the day. I remember driving from the southside of town to the westside, leaving work and picking up my children from school. I did not feel to go to group but decided to make a milkshake and not sit down for one minute. Mabel Manning Library was only a five-minute drive from my house. Never did I imagine that that choice I made that day would effect my entire life.

Wings from the Westside became one of my most popular pieces. I was in Elkhart Indiana, working with our daycare when for nights I could hear birds flying in the air. But there were no birds outside... and I began to write words as they came to me. The piece described my history and of most of the people in my environment "they had no fathers and those who were not able to share with them wisdom, knowledge and understanding" because of drugs and alcohol.

Ocean Tides was a piece that was sporadically dropped in my spirit. In this instance, I could hear waves. Nevertheless, I would always hear waves and words at inconvenient times such as while checking out at a grocery store or taking care of one of my children. One day I decided to purchase a mini tape recorder (phones did not record then) and as I was driving to Elkhart, Indiana, I could hear the waves again. I proceeded to record my feelings. Months later, it was published with JOT. Today, this is what TD Jakes would refer to as "Instincts."

The Beating of Drums were in my hearing at night as I attempted to go to bed. I literally, could not rest. I began to write about the message that was given me and afterwards I would fall fast asleep. This occurred for three nights, days apart. Africa a Reunion was also a popular piece that I recited in libraries and churches. Part 2 was published in JOT. The time of these poems was a critical time for me as a wife. My husband, Joseph, was flourishing in his calling as an apostle. He was sometimes away for 3 to 4 months before we were united. Occasionally I joined him in Cape Town, or he would return to the US. In these writings I believed that soon there would be a time that my entire family would join him. My premonition was prophetic because in 2012, the children and I flew together to that destination. We were greeted at the airport by Joseph and at least one hundred African brothers and sisters! The children danced with African garbs and tambourines. In summary, it was a glorious celebration!

Another poem previously published was "Chicago - The Windy City" This was inspired by events that were occurring in Chicago during that era. The Westside was experiencing gentrification, an act where low-income residents (mainly African Americans) were being displaced from their homes. Many were offered vouchers to move in the suburbs which had proven to be substandard land compared to city property. Many residents did not want to leave their neighborhoods because this was the only history they knew. Nevertheless, they were bought and/or forced out and a brand-new Metropolis was soon erected.

Other works previously published by JOT and written by me include:

Fatigue

Rage

A Candle in the Dark

Meeting the Storm Roller Coaster Ride

The Rose

Bessie Collins / We Ate from Your Hands

Afterword

Although most of these works were written years ago, I hope that you found these pieces relevant for today. For many years, these writings were scattered in different settings that included my office file cabinet, my home file cabinet, boxes, and journals at home. It had reached a point where I had no intention of completing them to be ever read again by an audience other than my children.

In 2018, however, the Holy Spirit spoke to me and directed me to search for every piece and put together a book. It took months for me to gather the hard copies and every week I made it a goal to electronically format ten poems. After months of typing and reading out loud, I am confident that this memoir is relevant, and its publication could minister to others. Today, I am doing what I wanted to do as a child - become a Free Lance Writer! I am also in the process of composing another book entitled "Wings From the WestSide - Journal Thoughts." In this work, readers are encouraged to record their own writings and categorize their lives through the major themes of this book or make up their own! The themes are: Inner Transformation - Total Surrender - Beyond Borders - Living Vicariously and Rebirth

I encourage you to reflect on major happenings in your life through writing poetry, music, or any means of art. I believe that you would look back in your portfolio and wonder, "Did I really write or make this?" And the answer of course will be, "Yes! Your wings were developing as you were gaining momentum!"

Take care and stay safe!

Debra Stanford, PhD

Made in the USA
Monee, IL
06 May 2021